TWIGGLE

For Marianna — who
orbitates joyful dialogues
without a mmmmmble!
Best wishes,
Jim Boren
4 May 89

ABOUT THE AUTHORS

JIM BOREN is the founder and president of the International Association of Professional Bureaucrats, a group dedicated to "dynamic inaction" and "making the world safe for bureaucracy." His exploits include running for president of the United States in 1972 and 1984 as the Bureaucrats' Candidate and winning trophies for three years in the Gross National Parade. A winner of the Toastmasters' Communication Through Humor Award, an aphorism author, and creator of bureaucratic sculptures ("marginal works of art" that depict themes such as tax reform), Jim Boren is an internationally acclaimed humorist and public speaker. He is the author of *When in Doubt, Mumble, Fuzzify!* and other humor books.

BILL RECHIN is the cartoonist for "Crock," the syndicated comic-strip that features that swaggering Legionnaire commandant known as Vermin P. Crock. The exploits of Crock and his men are carried by over two hundred newspapers in some twenty countries—and Crock and Bill Rechin have millions of fans.

TWIGGLE

Jim Boren & Bill Rechin

WARNER BOOKS

A Warner Communications Company

Copyright © 1989 by Jim Boren and Bill Rechin
All rights reserved.
Warner Books, Inc., 666 Fifth Avenue, New York, NY 10103
A Warner Communications Company

Book design by Richard Oriolo

Cover design by Jackie Merri Meyer

Printed in the United States of America
First Printing: January 1989
10 9 8 7 6 5 4 3 2 1

Library of Congress Cataloging-in-Publication Data

Boren, James H.
Twiggle.

I. American wit and humor. 2. American wit and
humor, Pictorial. I. Rechin, Bill. II. Title.
PN6121.B67 1989   818'.5402   88-27860
ISBN 0-446-38085-7 (pbk.) (U.S.A.)
0-446-38086-5 (pbk.) (Can.)

Dedicated to the officious,
bumbling, short-sighted,
happy, self-serving phoney
bureaucrats of the world
who made this book possible...

Dedicated to
OUR LOVELY WIVES, 'ALICE and PAT';
OUR AGENT, NAT SOBEL; OUR EDITOR,
DAVID NAGGAR; OUR PRODUCTION MANAGER,
TOM NAU; OUR COVER DESIGNER, JACKIE MEYER;
OUR PUBLISHER, WARNER BOOKS;
OUR FIRST GRADE TEACHERS; THE
GUYS IN BUFFALO, N.Y....THE ENTIRE
STATE OF OKLAHOMA; AND
MILLARD FILLMORE.

Stupidity wrapped in the flag will prevail over wisdom wrapped in the law.

Attodawdle

(1) To delay something by placing it in the hands
of an attorney. (2) A verb expressing the practice
of attorneys who postpone everything by slipshod
work, lost files, inadequate or undecipherable
notes, and the inability to remember the status
of a matter.

BACKUPUNCTURE

The skillful insertion of a sharp verbal needle or other career-cutting instrument into the back of one person by another. Backupuncture is a highly skilled maneuver, and is superior to clumsily executed back-stabbing. Backupuncturists rarely leave fingerprints, tonguescents, or traceable tracks.

BEDBUGGERS

The special police, informants, or nosey neighbors who, by authority of the United States Supreme Court, invade the bedrooms of the nation to plant bugs or other snoopal devices. Bedbuggers are missionary in spirit.

BIRECTIVE

A divided or two-way directive. Birectives are issued by those who travel both sides of the street (in the same or opposite direction), speak out of both sides of their mouths, or issue non-positions in the form of birective positions.

BIZZIFY

To cause much activity without regard to accomplishments. The verb is derived from the ancient practice of some teachers who find time for completing front-office forms and reports by keeping students occupied at their desks. Bizzification is now common in all types of organizations.

DO
YOU
HEAR
A
HISS?

Never do anything for the first time.

BLADDERATE

v.—To drag out or prolong a meeting until it must be adjourned to accommodate the physical needs of the participants. Bladderation is often used by those in charge of meetings...who withhold a vote or decision until everyone will agree to anything merely to get out of the room. Most successful practitioners arrange for a coffee break to be held prior to bladderating a meeting, and some open the meeting by a detailed treasurer's report.

BLOCKSTONE

To bring things to a halt by combining the skills of blockheads and stone-wallers.

BOOBIDOODLE

A specialized type of nonsensical doodle.
Boobidoodles are drawn by boobidoodlators during
boring staff meetings, professional or technical
conferences, and committee meetings. Boobidoodles
usually reflect the boobiness of the presentations
made at the meeting and not the boobiness of the
boobidoodlator.

BRAYALITY

A marginal thought or minimal message that is characterized by loud, resonant braying. Brayalities are heard quite often during political campaigns, but they are also common in commencement addresses, broadcasts of sporting events, testimony before investigating committees of legislative bodies, and the exhortations of money-oriented evangelists.

It's hard to look up to a leader who keeps his ear to the ground.

BRRAXX!

A mental reaction to hearing a stupid pronouncement by a person who should know better. Through the disgust of a moment, the expression may be uttered aloud, but it is usually a silent thought. *Brraxx!* is a mental whoopie cushion.

BUREAUPHONIC

A word describing the acoustics of the bureaucratic way of life. The bureauphonic approach is more tonal than mental. Bureauphonics include the background sounds of an office ... typewriters, computers, telephones, paper shuffling, the mumbles of staff meetings, and the burples at water fountains.

COMPUFIB

v.—To lie about the computer "being down." Used by hotels and airlines that have overbooked rooms or flights, compufibbing is spreading to other businesses seeking a nonpersonal "fallguy" for their poor management practices.

Loopholes constitute the fabric of the law.

CRUDGE

To creatively fudge or alter information. Crudging is a common practice of elected officials, political statisticians, writers of corporate annual reports, and heads of state. (Crudging should not be confused with "disinformation" or official government lying. Disinformation is more clunkle than creative.)

DEFCONSEX

Group sex as practiced by defense contractors upon the public...with the Congress serving as the budgetary or Red Ink Pimpernell.

DIPTECH

A specialist in the technology of dipping and ducking issues. A diptech is a high-tech version of a low-tech waffler.

DRIVELATE

To produce drivel with professional eloquence; to express a stupid thought in the form of a profound statement.

Bureaucracy is the epoxy that greases the wheels of progress.

ECHOSULTANT

A specialized consultant who tells the client what
the client already knows...in the terms the client
wants to hear. Echosultants use dittoanalysis to
help clients gain support for weak positions.

EGOFLECT

To genuflect and make other physical gestures and tonal expressions of subservience that stroke, massage, and otherwise inflate the ego of the person to whom the egoflection is being directed. Egoflection blends well with toadalities (expressions of one person's toadiness to another). Egoflection is found everywhere, but it is particularly evident in the executive suites of large corporations, in legislative offices, and in all environs of the performing arts.

ENSUGARATE

To sweeten up a sour policy or a political position to make it more palatable to a gullible public. Ensugaration may be accomplished through the use of beautiful words, meaningless but well-publicized awards, appropriately selected and carefully timed expenditure of public funds, and the suggestion of full employment or high profits.

ESTROPPELATE

To prevent a lawyer in a state of rage from contradicting his or her own previous assertions. Estroppelate is a functional blending of *estoppel* (a legal term for a restraint against self-contradiction) and *oestrus* (a non-human mammalian condition of being "in heat" or in a state of sexual excitement). Whereas *estoppel* can relate to any person, *estroppelate* applies only to lawyers. The oestrosity factor is to prevent lawyers from inadvertently doing to each other what they sometimes do to their clients.

PAT PAT PAT PAT

...AND THIS GENTEEL PILLAR OF...

ETHICATE

To give an improper or unethical practice the appearance of being ethical. A common ethicating technique is the use of well-known and highly respected people as character witnesses for unethical practitioners. In terms of justice, ethicators take care of ethicators, while ethical people simply get taken.

EXCULPUTE

To program a computer for an acquittal; to get oneself or a friend off the hook through the use of a computer.

Bureaucrats make poor lovers, because they want to make feasibility studies at every step.

EXFRITTERATURE

A type of expenditure in which funds or other resources are frittered away. In government, exfritteratures are channeled primarily through partnerships between the Pentagon and defense contractors. Other agencies exfritterate public funds during the final quarter of the fiscal year.

FALPHONIC

The threatening and resonating sounds of politicoligious hucksters who peddle variations of bigotry for love offerings.

FEATHERHEADING

Management overload; the upstairs payrolling of more managers than are needed. Incompetent executives use featherheading as the easy way out of unpleasant personnel problems.

FLOATUM

Bubble-headed, free-floating ideas or marginal concepts that float around conference tables, board rooms, and legislative halls in search of some significant meaning to which they can become attached. Like soap bubbles, floatum floats with the wind, and tends to rise and swirl during heated exchanges.

In a bureaucracy, ZIP does not refer to speed or energy. When you hear it, cross your legs, and keep your back to the wall.

SPINNNNNN....

GLOBATE

To deal with the biggest of the big pictures. When a globator globates, the big picture becomes so global that there are no corners into which the globator can be backed. High level globators do not need to know the details or the nittigritty of the business, but low level employees need to know what they are talking about.

GOOSALITY

n.—The product or the event of being goosed in a directive or nondirective manner. Goosalities may be tender nudges that tend to move a person or a policy in a different direction. Optimal-thrust goosalities, however, can launch a person or policy in an unhesitant and forceful manner. Some historians believe that progress evolves from the meandering flow of events, but others believe that a forcefully implemented goosality results in sudden and easily measured change. (Institutional goosalities should not be confused with personal nocturnal nudges.)

HALLJOG

To move with speed, determination, and high visibility through the hallways and corridors of a place of employment with a file folder held high under one arm. The purpose of halljogging is to impress superiors, associates, and strangers with the assumed competence and importance of the halljogger. Successful halljoggers never halljog with a briefcase; a briefcase indicates the employee is arriving late or leaving early.

HUNKERFY

To shift into a mental or psychological crouch in preparation to jump in whatever direction may be best for one's career. Football players hunker; politicians hunkerfy.

Sharing ignorance may not lead to wisdom, but it spreads responsibility.

HYPERASH

A special type of rash developed by voters and consumers who get hot under the collar about the excessive hype of political campaigns, pre-Christmas toy advertising, and pregame interviews of sports andahhhers. Unlike diaper rash which is usually treated with powder and drying agents, hyperash is treated by pulling the plug of the radio or TV.

IDIOTOXIC

A policy, program, or concept that is poisonously dangerous because of the idiocy on which it is based.

INFIXLE

An inside fix. An infixle may be the basis for some insider-trading operations in securities, point-shaving in sporting events, and certain judicial decisions which are an illegal but established part of the criminal justice system.

INFLATUATE

To inflate an ego with variable gases. Politicians, traffic officers, and some judges tend to become inflatuated with themselves.

INTERDIGITATE

To interface the digital elements of the hands in a professional manner. There are two classifications of interdigitation: (1) *simultaneous interdigitation* in which the five digits of each hand are interfaced simultaneously, and (2) *sequential interdigitation* in which the opposing digits of each hand are interfaced in a sequential manner. Prodigious ponderers, professors, and chief executive officers normally mix the two classes.

If you won't follow, they can't lead.

INTERGROPE

To grope around in search of a satisfying or safe place to land. An intergroper may be a person who is seeking new employment by feeling his or her way around governmental agencies, businesses, universities, consulting firms, or banks. Low level job seekers tend to flock in the waiting rooms of personnel offices, but high level intergropers perform in legislative offices or at three-martini lunches.

INTERVOID

To avoid confrontation; interface avoidance. To wordologists, the syllabic elements of *intervoid* indicate the state of being between two voids. Voidal sandwiching is not only common in all types of organizations today but also is common in personal styles of management.

KNEEQUAKE

The state of being when a person begins to realize the error of his or her position on an issue. A kneequake may be sensed as an unusual weakness in the knees, and is accompanied by a strange feeling in the pit of the stomach. The kneequake usually ends with a buckling under or some similar gesture of acquiescence.

To kill an idea, never oppose it: "YESBUT" it.

LEGALDETOX

A program which teaches managers who are former lawyers how to stop thinking like lawyers.

LOOPISTIC

Denotes a lawyer's purposeful search for, or development of, loopholes through which to pull a client to legal escape.

MENTAPHOBIA

The fear of thinking.

Never threaten anyone who roosts above you on the organizational chart.

MINDCLOT

A sudden stoppage in the flow of thoughts. Mindclot can result from boredom, the loss of intellectual interest, and the replacement of thought processes by televized impactions of idiotoxic programs.

MOBIATE

To execute a 180-degree turn in policy while
appearing not to be making any change. (*Mobiate*
is derived from the Mobius strip, a one-sided
surface that is formed from a long rectangular
strip by rotating one end 180 degrees and
attaching it to the other end.) Long term
mobiation rarely causes rippling in the
institutional seas, but short term mobiation causes
some disturbance to the ship of state. Oldtimers
can implement a mobiation by redefining a
problem or mushifying its directional thrust.

MOLARCHEK

To count or explore one's molars with the tip of one's tongue. Molarcheking is commonly used as an aid to staying awake in boring situations. Skilled molarchekers can practice the art while maintaining an attentive facial expression.

MONOMENTAL

An adjective used to describe the product of a one-track mind.

MOUSIFY

(1) to respond mousily to a management problem...a skittering away with fearful withdrawal. (2) To accede to a proposal or recommendation that one does not like. Mousifying is a feeble form of knuckling under that is used by weak middle-level managers.

MUMBLESCE

v.—To mumble with resonant and poetic overtones. Those who listen to mumblescers are thrilled by the non-message linkage of words and beauty. A mumbler who mumblesces is at the highest level of creative and inspirational mumbling. A nonmumblescer, for example, might greet a dinner partner with "It's great to see you." A mumblescer might say, "To be in your presence is to be lifted to supernal heights of joy and inspiration... inspiration that rises from the depths of profound sentiment to the ultimate levels of communicative ineffability." Sincere leaders in the clergy, prospecting male chauvinists, and writers of grant proposals are noted mumblescers.

Born again politicians are those who just won reelection.

MUSHIFY

To diffuse the impact of a policy statement, administrative directive, or judicial decision. Mushification is similar in expression to a boxer striking a bag of mush. The mush gives way, but the shape of the bag is only temporarily changed. Errors implemented through dynamic inaction, for example, are mushified by the graduality of their implementation.

NINCOMPOOPIFY

To make a major blunder; to waste resources with brilliant mismanagement. Any person can occasionally poop off money or other resources, but only a nincompoop can nincompoopify. Nincompoopery is a life style; nincompoopification is a management practice.

ONSTOP

To continue the process of stoppage...usually at a constant rate of stoppage. *Onstopping* programs are similar to *ongoing* programs except the continuity is in the state of stopping instead of going.

OOFISTIC

The response to a sudden blow to the institutional or personal midriff. Abrupt reversals of policy, unexpected changes in key personnel in an organization, an elbow to one's stomach, being caught in an embarrassing situation.

Oootch

A dribble of soup, a glop of gravy, or a splatch of food that attaches itself to a tie, a blouse, or other attire. Oootches tend to increase in size and tenacity with the importance of the dinner or banquet.

When in charge, ponder.

When in trouble, delegate.

When in doubt, mumble.

OOPSIFY

v.—To make a minor mistake. Anyone can oopsify but only nincompoops can nincompoopify. (An oopsifier may spend 30¢ for a 25¢ newspaper; a nincompoopifier may spend $14,000 for a vinyl-covered metal chair or $7,400 for a toilet seat.)

POMPISTRUT

To strut with optimal pomposity. The skilled pompistrutter combines rumperatory strutting with posturing pomposity. It is often used to project an air of importance or authority. Some pompistrutters perform most effectively in theaters, at diplomatic receptions, or while table-hopping at political dinners.

You won't get lost, if you stay in a rut.

PRE-GOOSE

To give someone a slight physical or wordational nudge as a warning of something bigger to come. A pre-goosal warning is often used as a hint to friends or knowledgeable associates to take cover before something unpleasant is uncovered. Pre-goosal warnings may not be strong enough to affect the marginal thinking of Wall Streeters involved in inside trading or heads of state who insist on secret arms shipments. Sometimes, pre-goosals must give way to a kick in the pants.

REGUNUT

A nitpicking naysayer who disrupts meetings by incessantly quoting inhibitive rules and regulations. The regunut, like the cat that yowls at the door, uses regunutting to gain attention and establish importance.

RESIDUATE

To burrow into a fixed, immovable position while maintaining a very low profile. Residuation is a survival practice often used during changes of administration or during periods of shifting management. Most residuators also hunkerfy.

RESOSIN

Reliable *source* of *sensitive* *information*. Whether from the horse's mouth or other part thereof, the seekers or recruiters of resosins often enrich the negotiations for information with booze, sex, and unmarked cash...preferably off-camera.

Do nothing, but do it with style!

RETROANALYSIS

The analysis of past events for the purpose of finding a scapegoat. Sportscasters, bridge players, politicians, economists, and pollsters are outstanding retroanalysts.

RETROPUNT

(1) To kick back money or other valuable considerations, such as from a salary, an overpaid service, or a service contract. (2) A kickback, as in "to receive a retropunt" or "to participate in a retropuntal funding program."

TEE HEE

Develop a countenance that reflects your philosophy. Conservatives frown; liberals grin; radicals giggle; and moderates stare.

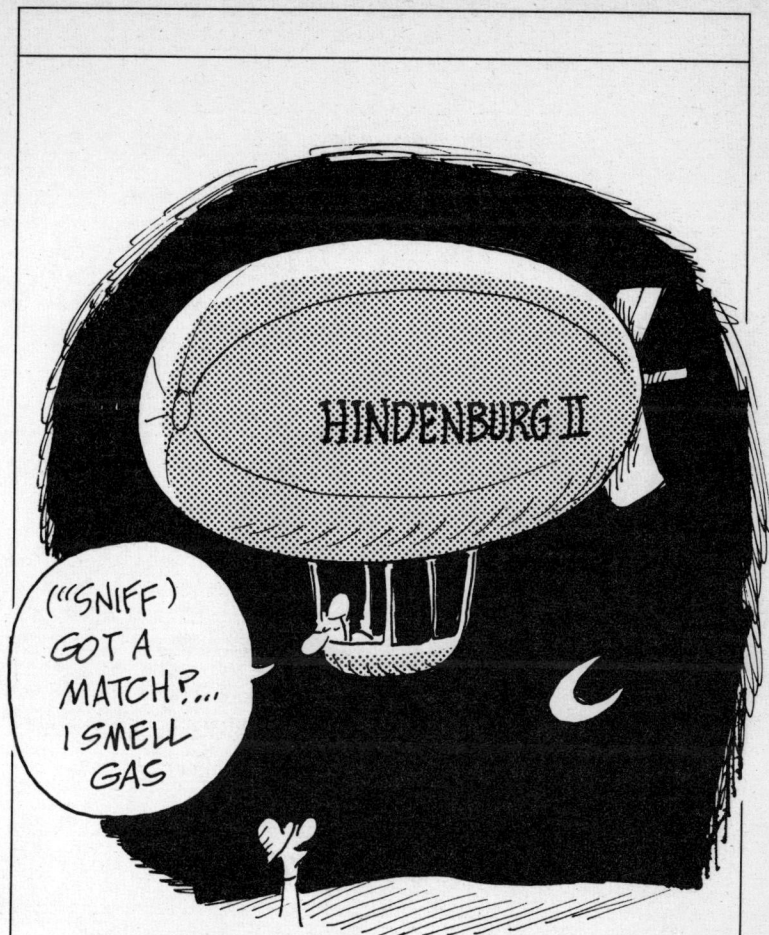

RETROSTRAGIC CLUNKATION

Tragic political or military failure based on ignorance of past mistakes.

ROSTRATE

To thunderate from a rostrum in a manner that optimizes flourishes and tonal patterns while minimizing transfer of information. Extended rostration often leaves listeners in a state of mental prostration. The prostration does not result from attentively listening to a flow of thoughts but from the search for a thought that may be hidden in the rostration.

Those who think labor is noble don't have to.

RUMPERATORY

A term that applies to the laggistic element of physical structures, logical abstractions, and other posteriorities. Rumperatory statements, for example, reflect the rumbleseat or afterthought of corporate or political leaders. Applied to organizational matters, the term refers to crisis-oriented establishment of blue ribbon commissions. *Rumperatory abandon* describes how many men think and a few women walk.

SCURRENCY

Currency that is fast-moving during periods of rapid inflation or deflation. Scurrencies scurry about the financial landscape of countries whose monetary policies are determined by votes rather than economic principles.

SLAFF

A strategic laugh. Used to: (1) kill an idea or proposal, (2) introduce anxiety or fear into a meeting, or (3) de-fuse a tense situation. When used by a skilled practitioner, a slaff can be a power control mechanism. A slaff may be a full and mirthful laugh, or it can be a sneering laugh punctuated by a scowl.

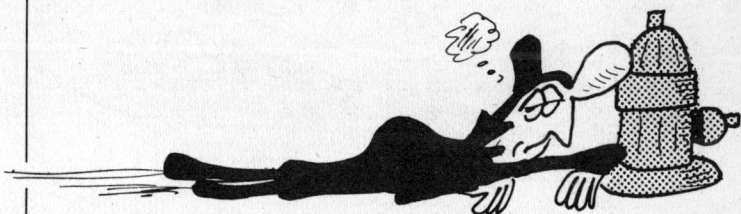

SNIFF
SNIFF

SNIFF

SNOOPIFY

To prowl nondirectively in search of whatever useful information or material may be found. *Snooping* is focused prowling, but *snoopifying* is random rock turning, bedroom bugging, garbage checking, and other invasionary practices that may result in informational leveraging. In the United States, snoopifiers tend to be journalists, political hacks, employees of intelligence agencies, and bedbuggers inspired by the U.S. Supreme Court.

SPENDAGON

Taxpayers' term for the Pentagon.

SQUATTLE

v.—To pass through a crisis or to survive a difficult situation by "sitting it out." Squattling is not to be confused with residuation, because one may squattle with high visibility while taking no action. Many squattlers squattle with resonant intonation, while others squattle with pompous posturing from a modified sitting position. Squattlers are known to be survivors.

TOADALITY

A word, action, or other expression by which a toady expresses his or her toadiness. Toadality involves the expression of extreme subservience, and it is normally directed to persons in positions of great power or wealth, real or imagined. A toadality may be a nod-and-smile genuflection combined with a slight secondary hand salute. It may be a quick rush to step aside or to scramblingly rush to pick up a dropped item. It may be an echoing grunt that punctuates agreement to some marginal thought. The range and style of toadalities are limited only by the creativity of the toady.

Being a little behind is better than being a big one.

WINESOP

A person whose knowledge of wine is surpassed by a pretentious and boring babble of expertise. Winesops, for example, babble about wines that "caress the tongue while being firm to the palate" and "offer a lovely nose...a bouquet of fruity excitement and ambrosial joy." Secretly, if given a choice, most winesops would choose a beer or a chocolate milkshake over a glass of tongue-caressing wine.

ZILCHIFY

To do nothing, or to convert something of value to a level of absolute nothingness. Zilchification as a devitalizing process is an essential part of bureaucratic technology.

If you've seen one nuclear war...
you've seen them all.